My Divine
Self

My Divine Self

Martha Thompson

BOOKS

Winchester, UK
Washington, USA

First published by O-Books, 2012
O-Books is an imprint of John Hunt Publishing Ltd., Laurel House, Station Approach,
Alresford, Hants, SO24 9JH, UK
office1@o-books. net
www. o-books. com

For distributor details and how to order please visit the 'Ordering' section on our website.

Text copyright: Martha Thompson 2011

ISBN: 978 1 78099 193 1

A CIP catalogue record for this book is available from the British Library.

Design: Stuart Davies

Printed in the USA by Edwards Brothers Malloy

We operate a distinctive and ethical publishing philosophy in all
areas of our business, from our global network of authors to
production and worldwide distribution.

CONTENTS

Dear Reader,

I would like to introduce myself as an ordinary woman living an ordinary life with ordinary problems. However, we all know that life can be overwhelming at times and can make us feel like we're sinking in quicksand. The more we resist, the more we struggle to keep our heads above the surface. It was at such a time in my life, when I felt I was almost submerged and gasping for air, that insights began to filter through to my consciousness. At first I was baffled, scared even, but when I began to find the answers to questions I was reassured.

I wish to share this treasury of insights with you and ask that you remain open-minded. In doing so you may find a way to avoid the quicksand effect. I wish I had accessed this understanding years ago; then I would have made a greater effort to live my life more purposefully. I ask that if you understand the message in these pages, that you would please pass it on to others, enabling them also to avoid the quicksand effect.

May faith and hope be your constant companions, and may wisdom illuminate your way so the light of your understanding can lead you to **your truth.**

Wishing you all that you wish yourself and more!

Martha x

Sinking in Quicksand

I looked into those tired eyes and it was difficult to recognize them as the once bright sparkling windows of my soul. A dim, cloudy rice-pudding white was now the backdrop of my jet pupils that once glistened as they caught the light. They were not jewels any more but more like dried-up currants. Where had that girl gone? What had happened to her? I really did not recognize her and I felt a great sadness at her demise. I choked back inner tears but they broke free and trickled down my face followed by a groan like a wounded animal. Why was I crying? No one was here to comfort me; I felt as if I was sinking in quicksand. My tears were wiped away brutishly and I found myself staring hard at my reflection in the bathroom mirror. Disgusted at the dark circles and wrinkles around my eyes and the unevenness of my complexion, I felt worthless. My entire persona was wretched and lowly. If I did not have an innate fear of suicide due to my reverence of life I would have thought it better there and then to end it all; to merge into the vast great nothingness around me. But then I saw my sister's face before me as a blurred vision and the chaos and distress I would cause her and others if I chose to exit this way. "God help me!" I wailed, as my mournful sobs gradually subsided.

Lathering my face with soap from a hand dispenser I then turned on the tap. I splashed my face with water a lot colder than I had anticipated which shocked me into the realisation that I had neglected myself. I had fallen out of love with myself. This self-neglect and contempt for myself had made me look and feel awful and it was taking its toll on my health. I had begun to feel pains in my chest and stomach. Why had my journey led me to a pitiful self? Then I heard a calm and clear inner voice say, "Come on Martha, take a grip of yourself girl," I felt compelled to repeat it out loud, "Come on Martha, take a grip of yourself girl." Then

I repeated it again but this time I shouted it defiantly looking back at my reflection with my hands clenched tight into fists at my side, *"Come on Martha, get a grip of yourself girl."* I then splashed some more water on my face vigorously and had a flash-back of myself when I was in my twenties. I was positive, laughing and smiling – life was opening up for me, I was meeting new people, experiencing new things and I had goals and dreams I was reaching for – but with the passage of time I had become jaded and disillusioned. Why? Had my decisions been wrong? If so, why didn't that clear inner voice I was hearing now stop me?

A sense of urgency suddenly welled up inside of me. I needed to grab a pen and a piece of paper. I dashed down the stairs snagging my skirt on the catch of the bathroom door. "Oh bugger," I gasped. I fumbled around my computer work-station under the stairs and found a pen and a pad tucked behind its screen. Great! I ran into the front room and threw myself onto my sofa, pulling up a side table in front of me. I was scared and excited. My heart was pounding fast as I scribed the stream of words that were filling my mind onto the pad.

My Divine Self

You create all of the choices around you by your actions and thoughts. They magnetically propel situations and people to cross your path, to enable you to initiate the changes you are hoping for. Your body throws out vibrational leads like fine silk threads that pull towards you all that you are hoping for, providing your vibrational wavelength resonates consistently at the frequency of that which you wish to attract. The more self-belief you have, coupled with the physical ability to work with any opportunity on a physical level to reach your goal, the more your magnetism increases. This will create and help you manifest the resources or people you need to assist you. Choices then present themselves to you, if they will aid you on your life's journey for your highest good. Even if the resulting decision causes hardship it can still be for your highest good, as strong feelings attached to any experience encourage you to take stock of your actions. You then draw upon your inner resources. This enables you to muster up gifts of the spirit such as: fortitude, courage, wisdom, discipline, selflessness, perseverance, empathy, compassion, sincerity, love, resourcefulness, adaptability, humility, gratitude, responsibility, patience, hope and faith. Hope and faith are intertwined.

Hope is the ribbon that secures the parcel of your dreams, whilst faith is the hand that delivers it to your door.

Both are the driving force behind miracles. So you must be confident in any difficult situation, and you have to believe in order to receive all that you need.

When you are at your most pessimistic your vibrational frequency diminishes. Negative thoughts retard your ability to materialize choices causing the vibrational threads from your body to lose their propulsion and magnetism. This creates a feeling of being trapped. This can be corrected by making sure you are eating a balanced diet. Drinking spring water, exposure to natural light, fresh air and brisk walks will also help to improve the sluggishness and vibrational frequency of your body. Repeating positive affirmations or mantras can override your negative thoughts. This will have the effect of changing your mood for the better and raising your vibrational frequency.

Without choice life would be boring and unchallenging. Experiences enable you to understand the possible repercussions that precipitate as a result of the decisions you make. Pain, illness, loss and joy break the shell of your greater understanding and these feelings remain with you indefinitely as they are absorbed at a soul level.

You have ears beyond your physical ones but many of you have become so bogged down with your earthly ways that your spiritual senses have become dull. If you would just reserve 10 minutes each day to sit in complete silence with closed eyes and simply put forward the following request, "What does my divine self need today?" then you would receive a stream of inspiration and guidance from your divine self. Your divine self is eternal and made of the essence of a universal power. It exists in spheres beyond your physical senses. It is omnipotent, omnipresent and omni-beneficient.

Acknowledging and reconnecting with your true nature on a daily basis will empower you. Life challenges will not seem insurmountable as you understand that you are Divine Beings.

The response to my cry for help was not what I expected. I had expected nothing. This need and urgency to write to myself was a strange, out of the ordinary experience. I had never even kept a diary. What made it more peculiar is that I felt compelled to read it as I was writing it. As I closed my eyes to go to sleep that night I realized more than ever that hope was very important. Without it I had stagnated. I had expected and believed that my circumstances would not improve. As a result I had made little or no effort at all, disempowering myself and so becoming a victim of my circumstances. I needed to accept responsibility for the choices I had made. By my poor thinking, I had also hindered the free support available in the universe to help me. Furthermore, the ability to remain positive in all circumstances was imperative.

More importantly, however, I needed to acknowledge that I was a divine being. This would afford me the power to cope and overcome any challenges that came my way.

I awoke the next morning and was showered and dressed by 7. 30 am ready to leave the house. I turned on my car engine and said my car mantra, "May I not maim or kill anyone today and nor them me," as I pulled out of my car space. It was a crazy thing to say every time I got behind the wheel of a car, but it did something for me. It steadied my nerves. I never told friends or family as I was sure that they would laugh at me. However, when I said my car mantra that morning I had a vision of the universe cocooning me in an ethereal metallic network of webs that was impenetrable. These spun out from my car diverting any unsafe drivers away from my path. I drew similarities to those extraordinary scenes you see in science fiction films, if you know what I mean. I found myself smiling from the inside out. I felt extremely safe and very reassured.

I was sitting at my office desk by 8. 00 am and I found myself thinking, "Same old shit, day in day out." My trail of thought then abruptly stopped. I was horrified. "Same old shit, day in day out" implied laborious tasks, the ingratitude of others, being dumped on, sorting out other people's mistakes, receiving no acknowledgement and no rewards. Without question my work colleagues had been facilitating my expectations to the MAX! I shook my head from side to side with indignation at what had resulted due to my thinking. The penny had finally dropped!

Dissatisfaction

Sometimes I would wish I was someone else. Then I had another thought – I've never won anything even though I am a kind and generous person! Boy, am I unlucky or what? I could sense a rant coming on. Why do some people have it so easy? Why do whole nations suffer due to natural disasters or constant wars? Why is it that a lot of bad people thrive in life? A plume of steam then came out of the kettle, it had boiled. The click of the kettle turning itself off interrupted my rant. I then made myself some tea whilst grabbing a handful of custard creams and placing them on a saucer. Ravenously munching into one of the biscuits the sugar rush refuelled my rant and I continued where I had left off. We are not created equal; we should put up and shut up with our lot in life. I then felt annoyed because it did not `ring` true to me. This triggered a response like a bullet. "I don't want to put up and shut up, my life isn't meant to be drudgery, it's meant to have more purpose and joy!" I exclaimed to myself. Surely I had not pulled a `short straw` from the hand of destiny? My breathing became exacerbated by the defiance I was feeling. I wanted more from my life, I concluded.

Closing the kitchen door behind me with my right foot and balancing on my left foot I managed to carry my saucer of biscuits and my mug of tea to the living room, knowing full well that this childhood habit was not really acceptable. Sitting down I drank my tea and ate my biscuits. After the last involuntary rumblings of my stomach there was silence in the room. I found myself scanning the room. In here needs redecorating, a complete revamp. Everything looks shabby and stark, ironically like my life, I thought.

I loved being enveloped in silence. It was non-threatening and it created a vacuum between me and the troubled world outside. A temporary space inside of me had been created – a window of opportunity that allowed some of the clutter of everyday life to be removed before the noises returned. Words, like air bubbles, then rose to the surface of my mind.

My Divine Self

If only you could see the spiritual resources at your disposal you would never become disgruntled! They are available for you to mould like putty in your hands, to help create your physical realities just by right thinking and doing. You would never despair but would rise to daily challenges, seeing them as mere cracks on your path that you could fix or stride over. You have all the tools you'll ever need to cope in this life. You have not aligned with your life purpose yet. The path you are on is necessary but your impatience, and your intolerance of present circumstances and responsibilities wears heavily on your physical senses. This creates an urge to start assessing your life. As a consequence this will lead to change. Don't moan about this, as it creates destructive energy that depletes you; instead do all that you can to create the conditions in your life that you want, working with what you have. Then think it and believe it. As long as you work from a place of love and service you will align with your true purpose and find fulfilment in your life.

We are all connected by the same breath, we are all one.

Our actions affect our neighbour like a chain of dominoes collapsing one after the other. So always try to see how your actions can benefit not only yourself but also others, unconditionally. You will then succeed beyond your greatest expectations as your vibrational frequency will be at its highest. Guidance and support will ʻfall into your lapʻ and doors that were once closed will open. You will be able to turn your adversaries into friends.

You will have attracted the assistance of powerful forces in the universe all working for good.

You undertake multiple roles in your daily lives. Value whatever you do in life because your journey has taken you there. There is purpose and meaning in the daily tasks you perform for yourself and others. They keep the breath of the universe circulating and advance all humanity physically, emotionally, morally and spiritually. The hardships and deprivations some suffer are difficult for you to fathom. In your world there are wars and natural disasters that challenge those who are bearing the burden of raising and cleansing their vibration, and those who are indebted to perform acts of great service and sacrifice. Out of darkness light can appear, just as day follows night. Sometimes communities, societies, entire nations and regions have a fragmented vibration that has developed over aeons of years of your Earth's history through specific beliefs and actions. It is a negative and disruptive energy that has the potential to jeopardise the humanity and progress of a region's people. It's as if the people living in those regions are breathing in tar. This accumulated energy is so dense and heavy it implodes and is broken down by Mother Nature and the result is what you understand as a natural disaster. The elements of air, fire and water decontaminate, cleanse, sterilise and refine such vibrational energies. People attached to these regions have played some role in creating the imbalance of energies that has crippled and stifled their own advancement, either in their present lives or previously. In your present reality it will be difficult for you to appreciate that it is you who decides when and how you put right your actions of yesterday.

Your existence is eternal and is one of progress. It is hoped that you will through reincarnations decide for yourselves to always work from a place of love and service. For you and your neighbor are one.

The unconditional acts of kindness you show to others you will reap many times over. It may not be an instant return in kind nor from the person(s) you have served. Being offered a seat on a bus, not being made redundant, watching a sunset, words of encouragement from a stranger, being in the right place at the right time, finding a £10 note when your purse is empty, strangers offering you solutions to problems or being offered a lucrative contract. All are typical examples of kindness being retuned. Angels walk amongst you in many guises to protect and to help you readdress imbalances in your actions by giving you opportunities to raise your vibration, if you so choose.

Some people have a greater propensity for evil than others. This is through choice which has become habitual over many lifetimes. They may have material riches but the life they are living will always leave them feeling isolated, lost and empty. Love will be confused with lust. Relationships will be insincere and conditional. Any joy or pleasure experienced will be fleeting. As your existence is eternal the opportunity to make progress is always there for such souls to make amends. The `road` they are on will be more difficult the longer it takes for them to correct past mistakes.

You are all created equal but it is up to you how you choose to develop and evolve over each reincarnation. Once you choose your affinities and kinships in the spiritual world you then decide what attributes to anchor in your psyche in order to develop your natures in reincarnations. This then influences how you wish to contribute to the greater whole, the universe.

The job you perform is your service to your neighbour, your contribution to the whole; whilst enabling you to utilise and build upon innate abilities you have acquired in previous past lives.

The words 'gifted', 'talented' or 'a natural' are used to describe the actions of someone who performs a skill very well. They have mastered particular skills due to dedication and selflessness while acquiring them in previous lives. The job you do connects you to obligations you have towards others and them towards you. Also, the conditions, environments and social interactions in your workplaces enable you to gain spiritual gifts and overcome weaknesses in your character for the greater good of all. The necessary challenges will arise and these will enable you to grow spiritually if you respond to them appropriately.

I now understood that my life purpose (or that of any other person) involved us in roles that would enable us to use and develop our gifts and talents. This gave us personal fulfilment but also helped others in some shape or form. Additionally, whatever path we took and the roles we played in life provided us with more credentials at our disposal. It was also important that we remained gracious and correct in our actions and let divine justice intervene in situations where we felt we were being abused. I had heard the saying, `You reap what you sow`, many times before and what I had read was confirming this old adage. The hurts and injustices we experienced and dealt out to others were always redressed at some point. Everything actually balanced out perfectly. Our career paths enabled us to contribute to society, acting also as a terminal for us to reconnect with others to whom we were indebted and who were indebted to us. Furthermore, the skills we acquired in previous lives could be utilised again in addition to acquiring new ones. This explained why there was a disparity between our skills; some of us had selflessly worked harder than others in our previous lives, excelling in our skills to become gifted. I was able to conclude that we were all created equal but we then chose how we progressed.

My Family

It was early evening and I found myself looking at my Father's picture on my bookshelf. "Dad, I miss you," was followed by a heavy sigh. "I really miss you." I had had a strong bond with my dad and he was my friend. If I was having a bad day, just hearing his voice would dispel any dread or anxiety. "What are you worrying about, Martha? Tomorrow can take care of itself," he would say. He would then brag and say, "I've never had a headache in my life, stop worrying. I'll have to get you some tonic from the chemist tomorrow." I was convinced that in my lifetime no one would love me unconditionally as my father did. My mother had died of cancer when I was nine years old and he had raised my sister and me as a lone parent. We missed him terribly.

The telephone rang. It was my sister. "Martha, have you cooked anything for dinner yet?" "No," I replied. "Come and have dinner with me and Daniel, he's missed you. He used his potty three times today, come over and give him a sticker. I've cooked more than enough." "Ok, thanks," I replied. I put the phone down and thought how fortunate I was having my big sister living six doors away from me. The invitation was a Godsend. I did not fancy having to cook something to eat that evening; anyway it would have been some type of junk food. I had lived in close proximity to my sister for all but five years of my life, so we were very close.

I came back exhausted as I had entertained Daniel to give my sister a break. She was a single mom. I had been his climbing frame, his helicopter, his action figure, nursemaid, story-teller and magician. He had fallen asleep under the red magic blanket. Hallelujah! How I wished my imagination was as active as Daniel's. Life would be more fun, I reflected. We lose this ability when we get older. It must be because we let our responsibilities get in the way.

The bedroom door opened slowly and my sister bent over her sleeping son and stroked his brow tenderly, gazing into his face as if in a trance. She then kissed his forehead. "Daniel's great, I wouldn't change him for the world. I love him so much! He's really funny! I can see Dad in him. Can you?" "Yes, definitely," I said. We then both stood looking at him sleeping for a few minutes, in complete silence. This made the minutes seem a lot longer. We were both marvelling at how special this boy was to us. Our father had lived on in him and it was a comfort to us both.

We said goodnight after kissing each other on the cheek and I descended the stairs closing her front door behind me. I then walked six doors down to my own house under an indigo sky which looked like thick velvet studied with stars that sparkled like diamanté. I felt there was a presence at my side. Hopefully it was my father making sure I got into my own house safely. I entered my house and closed the door behind me thinking how blessed I was to have a loving and supportive family. Then, from the recesses of my mind, the Jacksons surfaced. I wondered what had happened to them. They had been a local family of five dysfunctional children. The parents were always fighting and getting drunk and the children were neglected and unkempt. Social services had had to intervene on many occasions. Rosie (their youngest at 3 years old) and Billy (aged 5) were both taken into care to be fostered. It had been very distressing for all the children.

I wanted to know how families "were decided," as some of us definitely got off to a better start. Also, it had troubled me for years that my mother had died so young, leaving us at 40 years old. I had wondered if she could have delayed her death. I knew it was selfish of me but I had missed her, especially as a teenager, and it was very hurtful when I was reminded by thoughtless teachers at school to give my mother a letter when I got home, about a trip or a vaccination or something like that.

I kicked off my shoes and threw off my jacket and nestled against the inside arm of my sofa. I covered up my cold legs with its protective throw. Then, placing two cushions behind my back, I made myself comfortable before reaching for my pad.

My Divine Self

This grouping of souls in the unit called the family is important. Some of you are not reincarnated within a traditional family. The state may have been your family. *If you see yourself as a seed then the family is the soil you are planted in.* The constituents that make up the soil depend upon what gifts, challenges, lessons, appeasements, and corrections you have agreed to experience or develop; these enable you to tap into opportunities and so evolve in ways not possible for you in previous lifetimes, and also to put right wrong actions. Some corrections you experience may be viewed from your earthly experience as unjust, unfair and even cruel. However, your divine self knows that the unjust, unfair and cruel practices you have dealt upon others yourself, you too must experience these. This will make recompense by allowing divine justice to evolve. Connections within the family group will be stronger between some members. This will be influenced by past life associations that have enabled strong bonds to form, bonds that have become eternal and unconditional. Other relationships within the family can be fraught with difficulty and pain. This could be caused by weaknesses in character and or past life resentments. Either way many opportunities are presented whilst belonging to this group in order to resolve weaknesses or resentments.

Often past life enemies will chose to reincarnate within the same family to encourage a greater probability of resolving differences. Furthermore, other members within this family grouping would have agreed to act as mediators to help the souls involved to try to resolve their differences and so dissolve past pains and hurts; thus the healing process can begin and forgiveness can be gained. However it is up to the souls involved to decide when and how they will act for their highest good.

You decide before each reincarnation what your life formula should be made up of, in order to increase your chances of progressing spiritually. This includes: parents, siblings, relatives, religion, location, education, health, race, location, wife/husband/partner, gender, sexuality, affluence, career and unresolved relations and situations that require you to make amends. Therefore I will repeat that you have all the tools and resources you will ever need to cope with your present circumstances; but it is up to you to decide how to think and act to achieve the most desirable outcome, ie progress.

A mother dying and leaving young children bestows on her family a challenge – the family unit needs to evolve. Maybe the father needs to become more nurturing as opposed to just being a breadwinner. Being left to raise children would enable him to develop this aspect of his nature. Perhaps a soul needs to learn to become more resilient, resourceful and self-reliant within this reincarnation. Therefore the death of a mother would provide such opportunities. Furthermore, past life enemies as children would have ample opportunities to co-operate and work as a team. In this universe anything deemed as negative can always be turned into a positive experience depending on how you internalise it and act upon it.

You have an allotted time in any given reincarnation. However, there are circumstances that could arise that would enable it to be extended. For example, a student who has been in nursery for the required time has to move on to junior school. But if a situation arose and the student missed out on some of his/her lessons in nursery and the skills needed for junior school had not been acquired, then the school authorities would enable the student to stay longer in nursery. But if the student was more able, then the lessons lost could be waved as he/she would have demonstrated a higher average in the lessons already taken. This would enable him/her to progress to junior school with the rest of his/her year group. This premise is applied to your life span within any given reincarnation.

It was difficult for me to comprehend that I had been instrumental in planning my destiny before I arrived and that I was simply attending a school here. Whereby lessons I had failed previously could be repeated at my request whilst I learned new ones as well. This enabled me to make amends for past hurts and injustices to others and enabled me to progress spiritually. This was how natural law and divine justice worked. This was accomplished by my being reborn again to live other lives and it was called reincarnation. Reincarnation was not a new concept to me as I had heard about it in Religious Education very briefly whilst at school and I knew that Buddhist and Hindus believed in it.

I recalled accepting an invitation from a friend to go to a spiritualist church. Reincarnation had been mentioned in the service, but I had not paid much attention to the service as I just wanted to see the medium at the end. I had hoped I might get a message from the other side. I remembered being very disappointed as there had been no messages for me. As a consolation I received some spiritual healing. I sat on an old wooden chair and a healer waved his hand over my head; then his hands swept down the sides of my body. I felt undulating waves sweep through me. It was an amazing experience. I remember feeling very different. The dross of the day I had walked in with had left me. My entire body from my head to my toes felt very relaxed. There was a woman sitting adjacent to me who had also received healing (from another healer), who had sobbed uncontrollably. My friend later told me that something had `shifted` in the woman who had received healing at the same time as me. "What do you mean something had shifted?" I enquired. "She has released a burden or experienced profound healing in her body," was her answer. I had been indifferent to her reply at the time, but now I felt like something had shifted in me. I was thinking and feeling differently. I had a new-found trust in the goodness and wisdom of the universe. If we could access spiritual healing from the universe surely a host of other resources could be accessed as well.

Health

I had just finished watching a medical documentary about patients in a hospital. It provided an insight into the many different medical conditions that existed. The triumphs and tribulations of the patients were also explored. It left a "lump" in my throat. I needed to count my blessings as there were some people destined to be sick due to hereditary illnesses or diseases that had no known cures. In the programme there had also been a devastated couple: the woman had suffered repeated miscarriages. It seemed life was being very cruel to them.

I wanted to know if diseases and conditions that could not be cured were some sort of punishment.

My Divine Self

When your body becomes ill it is signalling that some part of it is out of balance. Your body's natural defences cannot align what is out of balance until you address the malady that is causing the imbalance. If you ignore this call from your body to pay attention to its care then the illness can become more embedded. It then affects more than the localised area, ie neighbouring organs or a complete system. The body has a frequency for health and when you become ill this frequency changes and throws your body out of balance.

Hereditary illnesses are experienced by those who are carrying past life hurts, burdens, guilt, denials, fears and responsibilities they have yet to relinquish. They decide to reincarnate within a family group carrying the same traits that need to be healed. This provides support for each person to release these debilitating emotions by right actions and thoughts. Your thoughts impregnate your being. This causes discord or disharmony within the cells of your body. Each organ and system holds the residue of specific emotions, both of joy and sadness. For example, sadness causes the cells of your body to lose their frequency of health. This lowers your body's self-defence mechanism against disease. Poor lifestyle choices and diet are also contributory factors.

In most cases when a baby dies this experience provides a lesson for the parents. Perhaps about valuing babies and learning how to empathise with others. This may prompt them to do charitable acts whereby they think not of themselves but of others. Also, the unborn child could have decided to end its life. It was in contact with the spiritual world during gestation in the womb and whilst in a sleeping state. Leaving loved ones behind upon entry to the school of life is very difficult; therefore some may decide to return upon being born or whilst gestating in the womb. Additionally sometimes the parents can renege on the responsibility of the incoming child; they no longer want the lessons the incoming child would have challenged them with. This would have been renegotiated in dreamtime, as when you are asleep you can hold counsel with your spiritual guardians.

The pain, discomfort and injury you cause to others mentally, spiritually, emotionally or physically are always recompensed by you in some shape or form. It could be that you experience what you put others through or that some great sacrifice is made. However, you decide when and how the wrong will be corrected.

These are the workings of natural law.

I found myself rubbing and scratching the nape of my neck. "This bloody rash has flared up again," I said angrily. "I'll have to get some cream for it this time round." I then fathomed that it appeared every time I was overloaded with work. At that moment in time I had several reports to write. I needed to find a smarter way of working so as not to offend myself. My body had been trying to open up a dialogue with me about my health and this rash was one of its many calling cards! Another was a stab in the chest and the latest one to arrive was a burning sensation in my stomach. I had ignored all of them to date but now I knew I needed to get to the root cause of these symptoms.

I knew my rash flared up every time I had too much work to do. With the gift of hindsight it made sense to never let my in-tray mount up. I needed to work more diligently and stay in charge of my schedule to keep my stress levels down. Amanda was a colleague I had to work with at times when we had to submit budget forecasts for all the departments. In the last meeting she had taken credit for work I had done. The day before, at the end of the meeting, she had spoken to the Finance Director who had thanked her for suggesting some cost-cutting measures to increase efficiency. These were the very ideas I had shared with her a week ago. As I left the meeting I glanced briefly at Amanda hoping she would sense how infuriated I was. I had not spoken to her since. It was at that same time I had begun to experience stabbing pains in my chest. Amanda had been someone friendly in the office; I had often chatted to her and even went out for a coffee with her occasionally. Her deviousness had upset what had been a cordial professional relationship. The pain I was feeling in my chest reflected what I thought she had done to me. I wanted this pain to stop and that meant I would have to address the root cause which was Amanda.

It was 3. 30pm and I made my way to the drinks machine in the corridor to get a coffee. As I approached the machine I saw Amanda walking towards me back to the office trying very hard not to make eye contact. "Amanda, can I have a quiet word please?" I said in a non-threatening voice. "Yes," she said. She then followed me into the disabled toilet closing the door behind her. "Honestly Martha, I had not planned to go behind your back. I bumped into the Finance Director in the car park as I was leaving work; she had stopped me to remind me of the meeting the following day. She mentioned that some cost-cutting efficiencies would have to be made and it would be a challenge for her to decide where to make them. I then suddenly found myself repeating what you had told me. When she thanked me in the meeting the next day I wanted to tell her that they were your ideas but it all happened so quickly. I later phoned her and told her that they had been your ideas. She said that she would see you in three weeks time, as she was on holiday leave for a family wedding in Australia. I'm sorry Martha, I just couldn't face you. I was scared." Amanda was shaking and a bit tearful. I was relieved and accepted her apology.

As we walked back to our desks I began to gently rub my chest where my crew-neck top exposed my skin – the exact place of my chest pains. I had moisturised that morning and my skin was silky smooth and comforting to the touch. With each rub I could feel all the resentment and disgust I had towards Amanda dissipating. As I sat down in my chair I noticed that the pain had gone.

I then reflected on what might have been causing the discomfort in my stomach. I knew my diet was high in carbohydrates and fat, plus it was coffee that fuelled me through the day. Furthermore I had been stressed lately due to not working smartly – that was going to change! Could this be the cause? I promised myself that for the next month I would drink less coffee, increase my intake of water and eat a more balanced diet. Also chewing my food as opposed to gulping it down would be a good start. If I saw no improvement, I would visit the doctor. I had realised that it was important to listen to my body. To ignore it would be at my own peril; I had a responsibility to myself to take care of me!

Love

A highly irate voice shouted down the phone, "Come on, Martha, let me come over. We can sort this out. We've got a good thing and I love you, I need you babe," he said. "It's over!" I said. His sugary words were not having any impact. "I'm not going over old ground again. You need to move on, Anthony. I have. Enough is enough. Don't call me again!" I slammed the phone down. My temples were throbbing like they were going to explode and I was shaking; but luckily there had not been any hysteria or profanities over the phone this time around on my part. I had astonished myself by showing a lot of restraint. He was not what I wanted or needed at this stage of my life. I had wised up!

What was it with me and men? To date I had been cheated on, manipulated and abused but I had got stronger over the years. Anthony may have been an Adonis and a good catch financially but he was selfish and a compulsive liar. I wished I had spotted it earlier. I was not prepared to join his harem of women to be at his beck and call. He had told me that he was ready to settle down and his Casanova days were over. Just thinking about him now made my flesh crawl. It had been a lucky escape, he had been so alluring. I felt empowered as I had managed to stay in control. The old Martha would have been in pieces by now.

In the blinding light of day I had to ask why I was still single. I was envious of friends who had been fortunate to find `The One` without ever having to really search for him. He had literally been delivered to them, so to speak, through introductions. While I `trod the tracks` ie frequented the clubs and the wine bars. Recently I had resorted to using the internet – for my last two relationships. But I was still a single woman, pushing forty, worried about being left on the shelf. Was I ever going to find `The One`, my perfect soul mate? How would I know? What if I was not entitled to love?

I looked at my bedside clock; it was 11. 50pm and I had to get up at 6. 00am. Time to sleep, I thought, turning off the light. I awoke at 5. 00am and wrote the following:

My Divine Self

Unconditional humanity – ie goodness, kindness, care, compassion, selflessness and devotion – explain the qualities of love. Without this essence in the universe there would be no bonds, no affinities, no associations and no progress.

It is the universal cement that holds us all together and aids progress throughout the universe.

We all have this essence but it becomes diluted by self-interests, fears and insecurities. When you are loved you feel joyous, blissful and safe because at that moment you are sharing from a universal reservoir of this essence that is created by us all.

Love is often misconstrued and used manipulatively for selfish means to control or possess others, to then take advantage of their insecurities and fears. *Love and know thyself and never compromise your highest good.* These attributes are important in your evolution and until they are acquired what you experience as love will not be love. You will attract teachers in many forms such as spouses, siblings, friends, children and associates who will challenge you to apply these precepts in your life. Experiences attached to suffering enable you to learn the lesson as quickly as possible in order for you to progress. The negative expectations you have of relationships become firmly anchored in your thoughts. You then magnetically draw towards you these types of relationships until you learn what it is to be loved and how to love another without compromising your highest good.

We all have ample opportunities to receive and to give love. Many of you cherish animals. The ones that live in close proximity with you regularly furnish you with unconditional love. They radiate their adoration and love for you. Their energy field becomes so connected with you that they feel what you feel. They selflessly absorb negative vibrations from you in a bid to heal and balance you. They sacrifice their own health to maintain yours. They are natural tranquilisers when they are loved; having the ability to dissipate worry, to bring you to a state of `sweet` surrender. The love from any animal connects you to the universal reservoir of love. They are magnetisers of this unconditional love energy. This explains why it is hard to resist not touching or stoking animals when in their company.

A soul mate relationship exists where there is a strong affinity and bond. Soul mate assistance becomes available when a soul is trying to make progress in a reincarnation and requests support in the school of life. This could be to provide moral support to overcome character weaknesses or to join forces in a project to aid humanity. This enables the abilities of individuals to be optimised for the greater good of all.

Such soul mate partnerships are behind the many respected and celebrated institutions that exist to provide and support the vulnerable, needy and sick. Such partnerships also help you celebrate and share your talents. They create and pay homage to all the healing, good and beauty you can create in your world to advance your civilisation.

In the spiritual world you make progress by developing your virtues and sharing your talents or gifts with others. This is achieved by advancing up a hierarchical structure of groups. You are mentored from teachers belonging to the group to which you want to progress. Upon being reincarnated you are asked to demonstrate the virtues you wish to acquire whilst paying off karmic debts (righting the wrongs of past actions in previous lives). Upon death and entering the spiritual world you are then assessed. This is to see if you have made enough progress to enter at a higher level than you were previously on this hierarchy of progress.

I began to reminisce about the men I had had relationships with and the associated pains and disappointments also surfaced. The more I interpreted the feelings attached to each man, the more I realised that each one of them had identified weaknesses and strengths in my character that would have lain dormant had I not met them. I likened my relationship history to me being a baton in a relay race being passed to each successive runner that represented a boyfriend. Sometimes the baton (me) got dropped. The heartache experienced in those relationships had been very difficult. However, I had been able to work through those feelings to move on to new relationships and over time my relationships had improved. Some boyfriends had become friends as I could not imagine them becoming my life partner.

In a relay team each runner contributes to the outcome of the race and in comparison all my relationships had contributed to my present emotional maturity. I had learned to stand up for myself through living with boundaries that needed to be respected. I also knew I wanted to be loved unconditionally. My boyfriends had been my teachers. They had taught me self-love and how to love others who were not family members unconditionally.

I was now at a point in my life where I could offer another person exactly what I wanted from them in a relationship. I had grown immensely. Everything was going to balance out perfectly! 'The One` would come into my orbit soon. I was just waiting for him to make the grade. Real love was worth waiting for and I would recognise it now.

It was also becoming clear to me that everything about living was about bringing out the best in ourselves selflessly and unconditionally. This scared me and I didn't want to admit to myself why.

Money

I couldn't help noticing that I had more silver threads of hair peeking through my black mop than I had the last time I checked, roughly a month ago. They had arranged themselves in two parallel lines one on either side of my head; beginning roughly from above each temple. I did not like this look. Cruella de Vil came to mind. I found some black hair mascara and camouflaged it, hoping that it wouldn't rain.

My finances were tight and had been so for a while now. I could afford the essentials but luxuries such as the hairdressers and buying things on impulse were now off-limits. My credit-card bills and loans were holding me to ransom every payday. As a consequence I found myself juggling my bills and playing a game that was back by popular demand called "robbing Peter to pay Paul." I hated it and wished I had been more frugal in the past. There was no one to blame but myself. I had a love-hate relationship with money. I loved it when I had it and hated it when it left me, as it signalled hard times. Yet I knew there were some people who had a great relationship with money. It never seemed to leave them and they could multiply it. They also had an amazing life-style to go with it, whereby all their material needs were met and no compromises were necessary.

I was questioning why this was so. Could I have a better relationship with money? Lastly, was money the root of all evil, as some people would do absolutely anything to get it?

My Divine Self

In the spiritual world the currency you trade in is good deeds. The interest you accrue is when your goods deeds generate further good deeds through your recipients. You have not yet mastered the use of money nor established a balanced attitude to it. For you it has become a vice. It is associated with contentment as all your material needs can be met through it, and so you crave it. Your self-worth is attached to it. It is important that you do not worship money but develop a balanced relationship with it as it has limited worth.

Financial limitations encourage moderation, adaptation, flexibility, humility, empathy and resourcefulness. Also, they motivate you to better yourself. You will then strive to develop your abilities. To generate financial security for yourself you will initiate new ways of serving others by developing new products and services. This benefits not only yourself but also everyone else as you offer more to society, enriching it and advancing it.

There are some people who are destined to have more wealth than others. This is necessary as it forms part of their "formula" in their present reincarnation. If you have less material challenges in your life the `gauntlet being thrown down` is whether you will share and multiply what you have by helping others, or if you will become conceited, selfish and greedy.

Money is not the root of all evil. It has a propensity for good and evil depending on how it is used and the motivations for acquiring it. It is a necessary commodity in your world as you have many vices. Money serves as a medium to exercise and purge these for the greater good, if your relationship with it is balanced.

I knew I had flaws in my character. I was quite materialistic and extravagant and I liked `keeping up with the Jones`; but now the Joneses' could jump off the nearest cliff. I was no longer fascinated by them. I also hated admitting to myself that this had been the second time I had maxed out my credit cards. I really needed to learn this lesson quickly. Is there anything else I can cut back on? Can I look for a promotion to earn more money to pay off my debts quicker and to save? Can I do a car boot sale? The answer to all of these questions I was asking myself was a resounding "yes."

I needed to work with money differently. I had squandered it stupidly for reasons that were nonsensical. Rectifying the situation this time round would take longer than I would have liked. The whole experience was humbling and I would never look down on people who were scruffy or unkempt. Like me they were struggling financially. I also found myself paying more attention to charity appeals on TV. There were millions of people whose basic needs were not even being met. My constraints were nothing in comparison. I had not respected money. I was determined to learn a lesson about moderation this time round. I would donate something to charity every month to remind me of how fortunate a position I was really in.

The wealthy have a greater opportunity to help others in society. By becoming philanthropists they would know the true value of their money and their role in society.

Religion

The sunlight streamed through the stained-glass window over my front door, cascading in blue, green, yellow, red and purple on the opposite wall. I was mesmerised by this effect and like a child I found myself naively stroking the wall that the colours were bathed in. I was ecstatic, glad to be alive even. I could not explain why this display of colours had unleashed a feeling of joy and wonderment in me. I had experienced this feeling before when I went walking by the sea, or on top of a mountain, when I sat by a glowing camp fire, or when I watched a sunset, or whenever a rainbow appeared in the sky. This feeling may not have lasted long but at that moment in time I felt complete and in awe. I had connected to something profound and spiritual, which bestowed on me an inner contentment.

My inner child vanished as quickly as she had arrived, as my present reality came back into focus. I could see a pile of junk mail on my doormat. I stomped over to the door. "More trees wasted," I mumbled under my breath. There were at least two menus and other promotions through my door everyday from restaurants, takeaways and local tradesmen. As I picked up the papers I noticed there was a brochure at the bottom of the pile. It was a Jehovah's Witness publication – The Watch Tower. I pulled it to the top of the pile. On the front cover there was a colourful drawing of a family sitting around a table praying. I took it off the pile and placed it on the bookshelf. I was not a Jehovah's Witness but it did not feel right throwing their literature in the bin. The image of the family praying on its front cover had made it sacred in my eyes, for a while anyway.

When my father had lived on his own, before he moved in with my sister, the Jehovah's Witnesses had visited him on several occasions. My sister and I were a little alarmed when he told us about their visits. Then we realised that maybe our father had been lonely in the daytime; so he had encouraged them to visit him so he could have lively debates with them. My father had been a non practising Christian and did not believe it was right to turn the word of God away from his front door. So even though he did not agree with the Jehovah's Witnesses, God's word was always welcome.

After several weeks the Jehovah's Witnesses stopped visiting our father. They had realised that he was never going to attend their church or be converted. However, I felt no malice towards them. They had been great company for my father and an extra pair of eyes to check on his safety. I believed that the Lord worked in mysterious ways as we were utilised for the greater good of others without really knowing it. Opportunities for kindness and service are 'interwoven' into our daily routines and chores so we can assist others unconditionally. For example, last Tuesday when I was about to cross the road, an elderly woman appeared at my side. We crossed the road in unison. She had mirrored my actions to help her cross the road safely. In my earlier selfish years, I would have moved away from such an offending figure. However, now I had worked out what the universe was asking me to do. This happened to me a lot.

I had been grateful to the Jehovah's Witnesses because of my father's experience with them. Their literature could stay on my bookshelf for a while. Maybe I would read it? I then found myself asking, "Why did some of us need a religion and why where there so many?" This had caused problems in society as each religion claimed to have the ultimate truth.

My Divine Self

Whilst living a physical existence many of you need a road map to help realign yourselves with some basic principles on how you should live your lives here. Religion serves this purpose and you are at the `steering wheel`. These different schools of thought exist also in the spiritual world and whilst living your physical life you may find yourself affiliating with a religion that reflects your innermost beliefs. These beliefs will affect how you approach the Great Divine, live your life and how you treat your neighbour. You then in earnest prayer have the ability to access streams of inspiration, healing and miracles from those who are in service to humanity through these schools of thought in the spiritual world.

Religion serves as a constant reminder that you are not alone. Others too have had challenges and have overcome them by serving the greater good by right thinking and doing.

Religion also helps you to live in hope and to access faith.

Some of you distort religion by your ego and pride. This causes strife and factions and leads to conflict. This makes religion "ugly" and its guardians and teachers misleading as self-interests are glorified and promoted.

I must admit to having a disingenuous relationship with God, the Great Divine. I only communicated or re-established a relationship with God when I was going through a crisis. During those times I would find myself praying fervently. At the end of it I always felt a lot better. Somehow I had found the courage to confront my problems head-on and work through possible solutions. There were even occasions when the solution arrived miraculously through strangers; even then I still failed to acknowledge the spiritual support I had received. I knew that if I had a friend that treated me the same way I treated God, either I would give him/her a wide berth or they would no longer be considered a friend.

I was glad I had an affiliation with a religion. It had helped me get through some difficult times in my life. Only now was I appreciating that invisible hands had guided me and brought solutions to my door. I needed to value my relationship with God, the Great Divine. I would pray to him consistently and not just in an emergency. I would say "thank you" for a change. There was no doubt in my mind that I had done a lot of taking and would continue to do so.

Animal Welfare

I watched in horror as, spurned on by others, a TV chef drank the beating heart of a snake that had just been killed in front of him, in a glass of vodka. It was meant to make him virile. His companions then ate the rest of the snake. I was outraged and shocked. I declined from cooking a chicken breast that evening and opted for some lentil soup and brown bread. The thought of handling the flesh and preparing it to eat just did not seem right. I began to wonder what kind of life the chicken may have had before it was slaughtered. It was not organic or free-range so it would have been in an overcrowded shed with artificial lighting more than likely; perhaps standing in its own faeces, unable to roam freely and breathe fresh air. Then I thought about other animals in our food chain that were also bred inhumanely, destined for our plates, such as cows and pigs. It had never bothered me before, until now.

The programme I saw unsettled me. I realised how much disregard we have towards animals we eat. We are their trustees yet we eat them knowing full well other foods are available for us to eat to survive. We are also willing to violate them in the name of science to advance our species. Surely our actions are wrong? I sat in silence with my pen and pad in my hand, with a reverence I had never felt before while writing.

My Divine Self

Animals such as cows, chicken, sheep and pigs willingly serve man by self-sacrifice. They are taken to the slaughter to nourish and clothe your physical bodies. As this fate awaits them they know that they are subservient to man and are here to serve you. They only ask that you kill them humanely and appreciate the bounty they are bestowing on you. They need fresh air, light and food in a natural setting in order to be at peace at the fate that awaits them. They also get reassurance when they are amongst their own species. If they are not taken care of adequately they get stressed and sick like you do. Upon consuming them your health will be affected. You should improve husbandry practices by adopting methods that enrich the lives of the animals that feed and clothe you, in order to safeguard your own nourishment and health. Such animals make the ultimate sacrifice to aid mankind, something which many of you take for granted.

Animals serve man and they are his companions. Your physical bodies need food to sustain them and meat is a rich source of nourishment which some of you will eat. Vivisection has assisted the advancement of medicine, and a greater understanding on how your bodies work and heal themselves. So here again we see animals being sacrificed to aid humanity. Man shows his humanity by the compassion and wisdom of his actions. When sacrificing an animal there must be rational thinking that justifies your actions, and the minimum of pain for the animal. Otherwise the slaughter is a cruel and malicious act towards another living creature and violates natural law.

With the growing population, our appetite for large portions and the acceptability of wasting huge amounts of food, farmers are being pressurised to increase their yields by whatever means possible. However, more and more consumers are in favour of humane farming practices to safeguard the health of animals and the quality of their produce. Also, an increasing number of consumers are also questioning whether animal experimentation is necessary. Things are definitely moving in the right direction. I only wish it was at a faster pace.

I began to speculate that a force for good would always

emerge to counteract a force of badness or evil in any sector of our society. Maybe it was a safeguard mechanism to stop us from self-destructing. It would also ensure that all our actions were balanced and weighed up without our free will being compromised by GOD, the Great Divine. Wow, I wonder?

Deceased Loved Ones

Sometimes on a Thursday morning I would go for a walk by the sea before I went to work. On this particular morning I noticed a very elderly couple pushing a toddler in a pram. From their ages it was easy to work out that it was their grandchild. They were doting on her and she had their undivided attention. It made me think about my deceased parents. They would never see me get married or have a child. It made me feel sad and robbed.

I often thought that my deceased parents may have visited me. There were several occasions in my teens when I was in my bed at night and felt the presence of my mother standing behind my headboard. Then there was the time at university when I was panicking before an exam when all of a sudden I felt like a cloak of calm and love had been wrapped around me. Inside I felt strong and stable; I could have taken on the world. I also recalled a boyfriend telling me one morning that the night before a face of a man surrounded by shimmering sliver light had appeared just before he fell asleep. Upon showing him a picture of my father he confirmed that this was the face he had seen. I was thrilled that my father may have been scrutinising my boyfriends but I was also embarrassed.

"Could the dead really visit us? If so why couldn't we consult them? Did they have the power to protect us?" I asked.

My Divine Self

Your loved ones are never far away from your side. They pick up on your thoughts and mingle with you often; moving in close proximity to you to calm you down with their vibration of love and strength. You need not be sad when loved ones die; they have simply shredded a heavy overcoat and have "moved to the room next door." The wall is heavily insulated but if you listen carefully you will hear them and sense their presence. It may be a feeling, or a happy memory conjuring up hope; a song, a word or catchphrase that enters your mind that you associated with them; or a craving to eat or drink their favourite foods. In all these examples your loved ones have drawn very near to you. They are trying to `snap` you out of a negative frame of mind by anchoring their vibration onto yours. This enables you to draw from the attributes they had when they were alive, such as courage, humour, patience and calm. This helps you cope with whatever is troubling or challenging you.

Every time you think of them you are literally tapping them on their shoulder and they respond by sending you encouraging thoughts when not in your proximity. If they cannot help you they will approach ministries in spirit to inspire you. In your dream time you often meet with deceased loved ones. Upon waking you forget so that you can get on with your earthly duties, take your lessons here seriously and remain committed. Many do not show themselves as they do not want to frighten you. They want you to connect with the living and fulfil your earthly responsibilities. In the spiritual world they have responsibilities to continue their progress. They can protect you if the need arises but be assured that you do have spiritual guardians who serve as teachers and protectors.

You are never alone. You have a team of helpers connected to a network of further support. You only need to ask for help and it will come. However, you have to be committed in taking the first steps yourself. Like a small child who is learning to walk by crawling, who tries to stand up but stumbles and falls, and then is glad when a caring hand offers assistance. This is the relationship your spiritual guardians and teachers have with you.

When I was down, I used to find myself craving coconut water – my mother's favourite drink. Upon tracking down a can of it, I felt comforted as I swigged it back. Now I know that my mother was imbuing me with her energy. She had been a real carer. I remembered as a child that a few coughs from me in the night would see me transported to the comfort of my parents' bed, much to my father's annoyance. I had done this often.

I found what was written very comforting. We are never alone, we all have guardians and teachers who inspire us and nudge us in the right direction. We only need to ask for help and actively seek to resolve the problems we are faced with, in order for the support to materialise. I now know why I did not feel stupid talking to loved ones who had died. They were listening and were capable of consoling me, even if I could not physically see or touch them.

Upon Dying

I used to readily kill crawling insects that crossed my path without a thought. Then I began to have incidences when I would be in the company of others and an insect would appear. I would automatically try to swipe the defenceless creature to kill it but suddenly it had a saviour. One or several of my companions would rebuke me, stopping me from ending the creature's life. "It wants to live too," or "What has it done to you?" they would say. The creature would then be picked up gently and released out of the nearest window or door. At that particular moment in time my shame consumed me making me feel no bigger than a pin's head, smaller than the creature I would have destroyed.

I now no longer kill insects. I let them go about their daily business like I do. Like myself they have a right to live. They play a vital role in the eco-system that supports all life forms including myself. What if someone 'snuffed' me out like that by clobbering me to death. How would I feel? Then the thought struck me that I could die at any time. I could go out for a walk and get knocked over, or collapse and have a heart attack. I would be angry, disappointed even, that I had not lived a fuller life. I would definitely feel regret, I concluded. My lack of respect for other living things that I had considered insignificant had been despicable; I was glad I was changing. "Do we have any need to fear death? Can it be delayed? Do good people go to heaven and bad people go to hell?" I wondered.

My Divine Self

Death is just a continuum of your existence in a different reality. Here you are not flesh and bone but spirit, an essence. You have the same thoughts and same ways, it is just that the curtain you were standing behind has been drawn open. The memories of all your yesterdays are restored from every reincarnation. You have a greater understanding of who you truly are. Some of you fear death as you give more importance to your physical reality than your spiritual one and your motivations are based upon earthly attainment, acknowledgement and worth. Many of the so-called rich are poor spiritually. In the spiritual world they would be paupers as they have not accrued any spiritual wealth. Upon dying these souls find it hard to disassociate themselves from their earthly possessions. Therefore they linger giving rise to haunting. They do not want to acknowledge their deceased state. For these souls dying is difficult; as spiritually they are `backward`, like a student dropping out of school and deliberately deciding not to take any more lessons. Very often it is their loved ones who coax them back onto the path of progress.

A call to return back to the spiritual world is heard by all those who are dying. Some of you would have been reconnecting to the spiritual world whilst your spirit gradually detached from your earthly bodies. You would have become more lucid and aware of deceased loved ones already in spirit. They would have been making appearances and communicating with you through telepathy. This would be to reassure you of your imminent departure back to the spiritual world. Whilst becoming more lucid and detached from the body a dying person can get glimpses of the future of loved ones they will be leaving behind; especially if they are anxious to depart. This will make the transition and letting go of their present existence easier. Glimpses of the future are possible as the past, present and future are all intertwined. Time is quantifiable in your reality but not in the spiritual realm.

Upon dying your spirit floats out of your body like a helium balloon taking to the air. In this instance you are propelled depending on your disposition into a vacuum of light and air, and gradually emerge into a space. It may be a garden, a room, a hospital or a sanatorium. There you will be greeted by some of your deceased loved ones, your guardians and teachers. They form a welcoming party. You will be encouraged to rest and to acclimatise to your new surroundings again. Upon arrival it is very difficult for many of you, as you are mourning and grieving your earthly relationships. A strong magnetic link exists between you and those dearest to you still living. You feel their sadness and they yours. So you are encouraged to send them loving thoughts and memories of better times to help bolster them up.

There are instances whereby people begin this journey back to the spiritual world and then are returned. This happens in cases when the physical body has experienced some severe trauma. This is because their spirit is `wired` to bail out under some conditions if the spiritual circuitry has been affected. This is dependent on where the trauma has impacted, but within a short period of time they are lodged back into their physical bodies. More than likely they will have some recollection of having been detached from their bodies, seeing brilliant white light and being immersed in vibrations of love once consciousness returns.

Heaven refers to zones of grace and enlightenment that you inhabit based upon your spiritual evolution. Upon death you gravitate to a zone based upon your spiritual credentials. Zones of grace progress onto zones of enlightenment. These lead to greater service to the universe.

Each zone is immensely beautiful. Some lower zones of grace resemble the most beautiful scenic sights you might see on Earth. However colours are a lot more vivid and brighter than what you are familiar with. Valleys laced with flowers that bloom all year round with fragrances that make you want to smile with joy. Mountains, waterfalls, sandy beaches, amazing blue skies and "mother of pearl" rays of sunlight. Sunsets of flaming reds, pinks, peaches, violets and golden yellows far more beautiful than your earthy eyes could ever imagine.

The more evolved you are spiritually the more beautiful your spiritual terrain and territory. You decide what type of home you live in. You create the castle of your dreams using your thoughts.

The more elevated zones, those of enlightenment, are bathed in a beautiful crystal white light and those who inhabit these zones have vibrations and natures far more refined and less dense than the occupants on the lower zones. Therefore if you are of a lower spiritual evolvement you can not inhabit a zone that is more evolved than your station. More evolved beings do enter and visit lower zones to offer support, healing, counselling, advice, inspiration and to educate others.

Heaven is a hierarchical province of spiritual progress dedicated to the good of all in the universe.

Hell refers to zones where the inhabitants are not motivated for the greater good of all. Here self-interests dominate. All manner of wickedness, evil, cruelty, vileness and depravity is the norm. Here the inhabitants are so far removed from their true natures of being divine beings that they have become spiritually retarded or spiritually backward. They have arrived at that stage of their evolution through choice, through free will. When a person dies and their spiritual credentials are not enough for any Zones of Grace then they will gravitate to one of the lower zones. Once again there is a hierarchy of zones relating to the degree of spiritual backwardness (evil) to which the person has descended.

The inhabitants of these zones have rudimentary, crude, hideous, gruesome and ghastly features. They are far removed from their divine natures. These zones are dark, dank, repugnant, clammy, humid, wet, warm and even hot. If light is to be found in any of these zones it is a murky dark yellow. Vegetation can be found in some of these zones and many are wilderness. Many of the inhabitants are in bands that enslave others who are weaker. Yet there are missions to save such souls. *Nothing is `cut off` from the Great Divine. "Rescuers," elevated souls from higher Zones of Grace, descend into these zones upon hearing cries for redemption.* They help to rehabilitate such souls when they request help to get back on the path of spiritual progress. Additionally, loved ones in higher Zones of Grace who have a connection with the lost soul will plead to them using telepathy to encourage them to make amends.

Love is the cement that holds us all together.

I now had no concerns about death. We were just returning back to our spiritual home. It would be like moving house to a neighbourhood where long-lost family and friends had already moved. Death must be a liberating experience, I thought.

Hauntings

"What do you think, Martha?" asked Ruby. "Wow!" I exclaimed. "It's a beautiful warehouse conversion," I added. "Ruby grinned with pride. I enquired how many apartments there where and she told me there were five. Ruby had got in early and had purchased the best apartment. She had a roof-top terrace which enabled her to see some amazing landmarks such as St Paul's Cathedral, the Houses of Parliament, The South Bank and the London Eye. "Are they all sold?" I asked. "No, one apartment was occupied for a few months but now it's up for sale because it is haunted." Ruby replied. Over the pasta lunch she had prepared for us, she went on to tell me that the owner had seen the shadowy presence of a man, that lights turned on and off, and that one morning she had found her purse in the fridge. So it was understandable that she was petrified of living there and had put it up for sale. There was a rumour that there had been some sort of accident in 1901 when a man had fallen and died. I asked Ruby if she was scared. "As long as he does not move into my apartment I can live with it!" She replied, as she poured some more wine into our glasses.

When I got home I flopped into bed. The wine acted as a great sedative. Upon waking the next morning and showering I began to think about the ghost. "Why do some ghosts terrorise their victims? How is law and order enforced in the spiritual world?" I wondered.

My Divine Self

Ghosts are human souls who have remained attached to their earthly environments and possessions. They lack perspective of their true nature and ignore any calls for them to reintegrate back into the spiritual world so their progress can be assessed. They still have their earthly habits. So if they were vile and evil in life they will also be so in death. If you enter their territory they will prey on you. You will feel uncomfortable when they are in close proximity to you. You have an urgency to leave the area you are in. Your protection will be assisted by your own spiritual guardians.

Ghosts have the ability to lock into your spiritual circuitry depleting your energies and disorientating you. They also have the ability to read your thoughts, sensing all your fears and insecurities. They will then prey upon these. If you have a weak moral disposition your vibration may be similar to theirs. This will make your resistance to their interference less effective. In this case spiritual armour would have to be sought from a spiritual teacher or facilitator, such as a priest or medium. This would serve as an opportunity to reform the ghost by getting it to acknowledge its state and to pass over.

There are some ghosts whose natures are very cruel and vile who congregate together to deliberately disrupt and disturb the living. If there is a chink in your moral armour this will be the doorway though which they enter. Alternatively a haunting can arise from an unresolved past-life situation with an enemy. A resolution would be possible if a medium or priest was to act as an arbitrator.

Hope is ever present to correct grievances, and for healing to take place you have eternity. For disruptive forces, there is also `policing` – just like you have on your plane. However, it serves to watch, monitor and to protect for the greater good.

I contacted Ruby the next day to encourage her to tell her neighbour to seek the assistance of a priest, religious teacher or someone from a spiritualist church. They could try to communicate with the ghost and hopefully get him to move on. Maybe it was a call for help from the ghost, I insisted. Ruby listened attentively over the phone. She said that there was a possibility that she might bump into the neighbour at an art gallery event later that evening. If she did then she would pass on my advice.

Ruby called me several weeks later to say her neighbour had not managed to sell the apartment and had enlisted the help of a medium from a spiritualist church. He had then successfully communicated with the ghost helping him to move over. Her neighbour was delighted that she could now live in her apartment ghost-free. As a thank you she had bought me a bottle of wine.

When Ruby popped over to deliver the wine I realised the importance of helping others unconditionally, especially those who I did not know. Over the last year or so I had become quite indifferent towards the struggles of others. My excuse was I had my own problems to cope with. Helping Ruby's neighbour to solve the problem of the ghost had made me feel really good inside. Receiving a bottle of wine as a thank you was an added bonus.

Race

I had lived in London for twelve years before moving to the south coast. I enjoyed being part of the rich `soup` of people I found in the capital. London had a vibrancy I had never felt anywhere I had lived before. I would sit on a bus with my ears twitching like a bat, trying to work out what language people were speaking so I could decipher where they may have come from. Other clues were the clothes they wore, their features and their behaviour. It fascinated me and I relished having friends from different cultures. However, I always questioned why we were not just created as one race, as there would then be more harmony in the world.

My Divine Self

Based upon the evolution of your planet, its climate and the development and adaptation of your species, it has given rise to many hybrids of mankind. This accounts for more than one race on your planet. No race is superior to the next. What matters is what you learn and correct through your journey of life in the body you occupy. Your race is just one of many facets of your life that equips you with what you need to make progress in any reincarnation.

Your species inhabits the Earth as other beings inhabit other planets. Man has visited space and other beings also visit Earth. Like you they are curious and are growing spiritually and expunging lower natures. The inhabitants on some planets are far more advanced than you are on Earth whilst others are far more backward. This is to assist the evolution of all beings based upon a hierarchy of progress. The inhabitants of these planets are different in composition to you. Some of these planets are not accessible to man nor his technology. The senses of man cannot detect them even though scientifically you may be able to prove that their environments would support some life-forms known to you. .

On Earth the more able students go to the most prestigious educational institutions. This is only possible if they meet the entry requirements. Therefore the planet you inhabit is an indication of your spiritual progress. Less advanced planets are categorised by the degree of evil, decadence and lack of cohesiveness and care in their societies for the greater good. Hence spiritual backwardness predominates.

I recalled how overjoyed I was when the apartheid system was overthrown in South Africa. The world was changing for the better. Furthermore I would not have guessed that in my life-time there would be an American president who is the son of a Kenyan father and an Irish mother. How events were unfolding in society proved that no race was superior to another.

We are not alone in this big universe, other intelligent species exist. They like us are being provided with opportunities to grow spiritually. This makes good sense to me, as surely the other planets are not in space just for decoration.

Plastic Surgery

I had begun to notice more than ever as I approached my late 30s that the shape of my body was changing. My hips, thighs, legs and arms had become thicker and fatter. I also noticed that I had a "muffin-top" stomach that readily hung over my waistband especially when I wore trousers. So I had given up wearing them as they seemed to emphasise my metaphorism into this bigger woman, and I wanted to disassociate myself from her.

I had tried every crash diet imaginable but the weight always came back. I had exercised on and off. However, I had convinced myself that I needed to take care of my joints and therefore going running was out of the question. Anyway, I would look awful in a jogging suit. I would often notice the adverts in magazines about plastic surgery and think how easy it would be to correct my fat and thick bits if I could only afford it. This would preoccupy my thoughts especially if I had difficulty finding something to put on that morning and had left my bed `drowning in a sea` of clothes. If I had a spare £10,000 I would pay for surgery to correct my body, I concluded. When I had spoken to my sister about this topic she thought it was immoral. Who was right?

My Divine Self

The body you occupy is a sacred vessel which needs nourishment and care. If you abuse it this triggers degenerative processes which prevent its ability to function optimally. Additionally its natural defences are weakened and disease can then become embedded. Vanityand laziness have led you to seek out surgery. A change in diet, an exercise regime, genuine respect for your body and self-discipline rather than gluttony would see you mastering your weight issue. You need to develop a different relationship with food by seeing it as a fuel. The better the fuel, the better the body will function. Plying yourself with excessive carbohydrates and fats as opposed to a balanced input of nutrients has contributed to your excessive weight gain. Until you rethink your relationship with food and actively take care of your body your weight issue will persist. This will then cause further health issues which will impair the quality of your life. When you are upset, disappointed or bored and find yourself eating to fill the void or to dispel the sadness that envelopes you, say this affirmation:

"I love my body and I am taking care of it by eating in a balanced way." Then see yourself in a leaner and fitter body looking healthy and well. The need to reach for food to soften life's knocks will diminish the more you practice saying this affirmation.

Surgery would successfully alter your physical body but you are much more than flesh and bone. The surgeon's scalpel would not have altered your emotional, mental and spiritual bodies that are interlaid around your physical body, that which holds the template of your physical form. For these bodies to alter, and to keep off the weight, there would have to be some changes in your eating habits and thought patterns. Otherwise the weight would return. Also, if damage occurred in the physical body during surgery preventing further fat being deposited in the areas that were removed, then future fat would deposit itself in other parts of the body not ideally suited for its storage. This would cause an imbalance, creating a strain on organs and systems in the body that normally would not be affected by fat deposits. You would have created further and more damaging effects to your body. Many of you are in a vicious cycle with food, having failed to take responsibility for the welfare of your bodies. You have not taken active steps to change your thinking, lifestyle and eating patterns.

Plastic surgery helps to improve emotional scars and insecurities caused by disfigurements by the acts of others, accidents and from birth defects. It is a medical advancement to help you heal yourselves and is not immoral. However, it has been abused and misused for vanity's sake; this does nothing to improve you but depreciates your spiritual worth.

If I continued to neglect the care of my body by a wrong diet and by making poor life choices the quality of my life would get worse over time. I could begin by taking small steps. Eating on a smaller plate and making sure I ate a variety of foods. I would get a book from the library on nutrition to re-educate myself about healthy eating. Also, I knew there were a lot of healthy diet plans and information I could access off the internet. The bed-sheet covering my cross-country trainer in the spare bedroom would be removed. I needed to start using it again.

Drugs and Alcoholism

My day had been very stressful and upon opening the fridge door I grabbed a chilled bottle of white wine. Finding a corkscrew I carefully opened the bottle and poured a large quantity of it into one of my giant pink wine glasses. It trickled down my throat like liquid mercury and before I knew it the glass was empty. I poured another and again I consumed it very quickly. Then I poured another. Within a short time I could feel the alcohol taking effect. Instinctively I found myself holding back from swallowing any more wine, it was an unconditional response.

When I was at university I had got violently drunk. The morning after I had vowed I would never get drunk again. The entire hall of residence had heard my vomiting episode at 3. 00 am which had left me embarrassed and feeling very ill. This probably explained why I had the self-discipline not to get inebriated ever again. The experience had left a lasting impression.

As a small child I was asthmatic and the smell of cigarettes or any kind of smoke irritated me. So as an adult I still had a dislike for any type of smoke as previously it may have triggered off an asthmatic attack. Furthermore I could not understand why anyone would want to breathe in smoke or loose control of their senses by taking hallucinogenic substances. Yet I had friends who looked forward to getting drunk and taking drugs at the weekend. They said it was fun, exhilarating and it relaxed them.

As I put a stopper in the wine bottle and placed it back into the fridge, I pondered why some of us have a greater tendency for getting drunk and taking drugs than others.

My Divine Self

Some people have a propensity to throw themselves away in complete abandonment by using drugs and or alcohol; they want to suppress their personal worries and cares and to nullify their senses. This enables them to negate their responsibilities. The burdens of the material world bear down heavily on them making it difficult for them to seek the support they need and to achieve balance in their lives. They would have faced the same or similar cravings in previous lifetimes.

You are responsible for your own growth towards spiritual maturity whilst on Earth and many of you sabotage your progress by not confronting your fears or putting things into perspective. Until a lesson is learned it will constantly be repeated in reincarnations in various guises.

Like students in a classroom following a course of study you cannot progress to the next level of your studies unless you have passed all the modules in your present line of study.

Fortunately my medical disposition as a child had made some recreational life-style choices undesirable to me. My first drunken experience had made me reassess my relationship with alcohol. I had chosen to approach it with caution and never to drink myself into a stupor. I was glad this was one less vice I had to worry about in this lifetime.

Anxiety and Restlessness

What was wrong with me today? I had been like a bear with a sore head. I was moody and grumpy, impatient and angry for no particular reason. I couldn't wait to leave the supermarket to get home and close my front door on the world. When I arrived home I unplugged the phone; I wanted no disturbances as I felt out of sorts, out of balance. Within half an hour I felt my normal self again but I wanted to know what had caused this inner turbulence earlier.

My Divine Self

If you have a sensitive nature you can sense and feel atmospheres and the energy of others around you. This enables you unconsciously to pick up on the vibes of others. You all emit waves of undulating energy that radiate out from your bodies; these waves are linked to what you are thinking and feeling. Therefore it is detrimental to you if you are around negative individuals all of the time. If you recognise this happening remove yourself and/or visualise yourself standing in an electric-blue coloured flame glowing brilliantly and burning off any dross from your body, as a black smoke blowing off you and disappearing in the ether around you. Or alternatively visualise yourself zipped up in a hooded cloak that is metallic sliver on the outside like tin-foil and electric-blue velvet on the inside. Then affirm, "I am safe and protected." This should be done daily.

You would have manipulated the ether around you by creating a shield using colour vibrations. Electric-blue combined with metallic silver is the colour signature of protecting angels and it is their vibration you are drawing on.

As long as your nature is not essentially vile, evil or debased they will never deny you assistance. We are all born with a colour signature, a vibrational colour frequency.

Your essence that stems from the Great Divine which is your spirit is of the appearance and nature of an ethereal gossamer shimmering light. It is more beautiful in colour than anything your physical eyes have ever seen; they cannot compare to colours in your physical world.

If our spirit is made up of light energy, does this explain why we all have a natural affinity to colour? No wonder I feel so elated when I see a rainbow. Does this also explain why so many of us love natural sunlight beaming down on us? Could it be that at that time we are connecting to the "source" and it is revitalising us?

Suicide and Euthanasia

Susie from the admin department had invited me out for lunch. Her face was drained of colour and her eyes appeared puffy and red. "You look awful," I said, gently rubbing her shoulder as we sat down. "What's wrong?" "It's my mother, she getting worse. I visited her at the care home last night. She doesn't recognise me. She keeps bumping into things and falling over and swearing a lot. I don't recognise her! I can honestly say that I had never heard my mum swear in all my life until yesterday." Tears were now rolling down Susie's face whilst I desperately searched for some tissues in my bag. Finding some I placed a clump in her hand and wiped away a stray tear that had rested on her left cheek. Susie then wiped her eyes dry and said, "I swear to God, Martha, if I get dementia or Alzheimer's I'll kill myself." I tried to offer some reassuring words. "I'm sure your mother knows who you are, Susie, and gets comfort knowing that you visit her. You're a good daughter, Susie. Keep strong." Susie composed herself and began to drink her latte. We did not talk much after her emotional outburst. An awkward silence followed. I would never `entertain` killing myself. I thought suicide was wrong but my `heart went out` to her. "Susie, call me anytime if you need someone to talk to," I said as we parted to go back to our different sections in the office. When I sat at my desk that afternoon I thought about Susie and the possibility of her becoming ill like her mother. I then questioned whether all suicides were wrong.

My Divine Self

Suicide arises when you descend into a state of despair. Hope has been lost, like a battery slowly losing its charge, and despondency is in its place. You arrive in a very distressed state back into the spiritual world. You may have taken on challenges far too great for yourself whilst reincarnated, against the better judgement and advice of your guardians or teachers due to your own pride and/or impatience to progress. Or, because of your sensitive nature, you found it difficult being reincarnated and wanted to bail out as opposed to trying again. Therefore you adopted a careless and reckless approach to your own care by leading a lifestyle that damaged your health – unconscious suicide. Whatever damage you do to your physical body will have to be confronted in another lifetime or lifetimes.

Some physical challenges such as illness or loss are hard to bear. Therefore some of you decide to end your life by your own hand or by the hand of others. You all have free will and the choice is yours. However, your bodies are sacred vessels and should be regarded as such. You are all here to evolve spiritually and your life experiences are your lessons. Many untamed emotions such as anger, envy, fear and greed as well as physical limitations will all be tested to provide you with the opportunity to mature spiritually. Nevertheless some of you will decide not to proceed.

Guardians and teachers who work with you in spirit often know the likelihood of your aborting the school of life through suicide; therefore preparation is made for this. However, if you constantly violate the sacredness of your life force due to cowardice, stubbornness, waywardness and irresponsibility arising from a frivolous nature you cannot inhabit the higher Zones of Grace as you do not wish to progress. You will go to a zone of likeminded others but the door to progress is always open to you.

Thinking back there have been times in my life when I wished I could have bailed out of situations in which I found myself.

However, due to my responsibility to others, advice received or in order to uphold my reputation I was forced to take stock and to persevere. When the challenge or difficulty had passed I was relieved to have seen it through. More importantly I could see now that I had benefited by not bailing out. I had exposed my vulnerability and confronted my greatest fears and insecurities. I had worked through them and had conquered them. If I had constantly bailed out of situations that I found challenging I would not have accumulated any inner resources or `gifts` to cope with future challenging situations. The most difficult challenges were the best lessons as they had taught me more and enabled me to bring out the best in myself. These were the gifts I had earned.

When it comes to personal growth nothing can be given to us. We have to work for it.

Angels and Fairies

As I was polishing I noticed that a glass wing had fallen off the angel ornament I had received as a gift from a friend last Christmas. I duly found some glue and mended it. That Christmas I also received a courtesy gift of a miniature angel teddy bear with a book I had ordered that had arrived three weeks late. I was not a cuddly toy kind of person but I remember looking at it bemusedly and hanging it from a curtain hook in the living room. I then received an angel key-ring from another friend who had visited Salisbury Cathedral. I recall thinking at the time whether this was a sign of an imminent visit from an angel as I never bought such paraphernalia for myself. I did not have a visitation from any angel, but I did find two feathers on the floor of my bedroom that were meant to be their calling cards. However, common sense lead me to believe that they had fallen out of my pillow or my duvet and so I dismissed them as being feathers from my bedding and not from an angel.

My friend Mary who had given me the ornament was fascinated by angels and fairies. She said she had sensed them and often found feathers. Her home was adorned with pictures and statues of them in every room, even in thebathroom. She said this was to encourage them to come into her home. I liked Mary a lot but I remained sceptical. Did they really exist?

My Divine Self

An infinite number of divine beings co-exist in spheres beyond your physical senses, each having evolved over aeons of time. They play a vital role in the complex network of development and support in the universe. Angels are beings who have a specialised service to perform in the maintenance of the universe. They are of their own order and are also of the essence of the Great Divine. They are beings more diverse than the human race in shape, form, colour and intelligence. They are beautiful radiant beings of great power and intelligence. They exist in ministries that are councils of service: supervising, planning, co-ordinating, educating, caring, developing, implementing and protecting. Each ministry has a speciality such as the Arts, Healing, Science, Fauna and Flora. Ministries exist for every region of the universe.

Angels also have free will. However, because of their evolved nature, many dedicate themselves to the service of others. They experience great joy and bliss when they see harmony and progress in the universe.

There are some angels who have misused they power. These once radiant beings of light and grace have coarse and debased natures and cannot inhabit the Zones of Grace. They have formed they own territories. Angels do walk amongst you in many guises. They intervene in situations under divine instruction to lessen the destructive actions of mankind; or when additional protection is needed to ensure a person's lesson in the school of life is not abruptly stopped. Those in the healing ministries often leave a floral smell representing the flora or fauna associated with their specific healing band (speciality). Others leave items that you associate in your psyche with angels, such as feathers, or signs you feel comfortable with. For example, birds, butterflies and rainbows. Most often their help goes unnoticed as the person they have assisted is said to be lucky.

Fairies are beings of their own order. Like angels they have a speciality. They are linked to the elements of air, fire, water and earth. They are assigned duties relating to flora and fauna and the balance of nature. Some are innocent, playful and naïve in nature like young children, whilst some are mischievous. They are clothed in the elements they serve. Very rarely are they ever seen.

You are never alone. You have guardians whom many of you call guardian angels. They are souls who have reincarnated many times on your planet and others. They have learned valuable lessons and have acquired wisdom. They can be members of your spiritual family, those you have a very strong bond to in the spiritual world. They participate in the internal dialogue you have with yourself and imbue you with their wisdom, courage, humour, creativity and strength to nudge you into right thinking and acting. Upon gestation in the womb you have guardians attached to you. They act as protectors and caretakers ensuring you are prepared to make the journey through to your physical birth and that nothing should hinder the gestation period while you are being incubated in the womb, if this is what is "timetabled" to happen. During infancy and through to puberty your guardians are quite often members of your spiritual family. Those you have a strong affinity with in the spiritual world.

Just as earthly parents are commissioned in most cases to oversee your progress, safety and care, so too are your spiritual guardians. In early adulthood more specialised caretakers intervene to inspire you in your choice of service and to help you work through any challenging karmas. So, for example, a person who is destined to be a doctor but who had a vice for hedonism from a past life may have a medic as a guardian such as a medicine man, or someone who belonged to the clergy (for example, a priest or someone who was able to demonstrate chastity or balance).

You all have multiple guardians. They join you at various stages of your earthly campaign. The number you have depends on the support you need and the level of service you are willing to offer to others. However, there is a main caretaker overseeing your progress and this guardian stays with you throughout your life.

When you are stressed or worried it is often suggested that you `sleep on it`. The gift of sleep not only serves to replenish your body, but enables you to enter into dialogue with your guardians, and get the advice you need. Your higher mind registers the wisdom shared to you by your guardians and your body reacts by being reassured. Therefore the burden that was there the night before, by morning may have gone or should at least be a lot lighter. You would have awoken with an innate knowing and fortitude that a viable solution exists.

Guardians are more often sensed than seen. However, a more sensitive or intuitive person might get an internal or external vision of perhaps one of their guardians who is working a lot with them presently. However, the majority of you will not see or sense your guardians. This is because the onus is on you to apply yourself to make progress during any reincarnation. Therefore the challenges you face are your own and only you can conquer them. Your guardians only serve to inspire, protect, support, reassure, guide and of course to love you unconditionally. If they revealed themselves to everyone some of you would seek to be indulged and could become lazy. Therefore your accomplishments would be minimal and some of you would give up.

So often I would frown upon vagrants and dishevelled individuals who sometimes would approach me for help when I was out in public places. Now I know I could have been turning away angels. I felt so much adoration and humility knowing that I had dedicated guardians looking out for me 24/7. I was also flabbergasted and amazed to have some insight in to how this giant jigsaw called the universe joined together for the greater good of all.

The World Seems Uneasy At The Moment

Watching the seven o'clock news was part of my daily routine. I was saddened as there seemed to be a lot of unrest in the world. Civil wars were breaking out in once stable countries in the Middle East due to people's natural freedoms being supressed. More dead soldiers were being repatriated from Iraq and Afghanistan to grieving families. Additionally people were losing their jobs and a global recession was being predicted. There had also been a tsunami in Japan killing thousands of people. It had left a trail of devastation. It had destabilised several nuclear reactors causing alarm throughout the world. "What if the unthinkable happened? What was happening? Why now?" I enquired.

My Divine Self

The Earth's vibrational frequency is changing. Your world is evolving and its heart is beginning to beat at a faster pace in anticipation. People are craving spiritual sustenance. Your divine nature knows of your interconnectedness with all living things but your physical nature has lost its sense of service to others as selfish interests dominate in many areas of your lives. This has left many of you hankering after something. For some of you this means going back to basics and living a simplified life working in harmony with nature, for example working the land, or having allotments or smallholdings. You want to strip away the material strappings of your lives as you feel as if you are in bondage. Others of you will be drawn to doing voluntary work in developing countries and poorer communities. Or the same hankering may have awoken the need for new freedoms and modes of expression and the righting of injustices. These feelings would have been amplified by your disconnection to the universal vibration of being all one. This has resulted in society becoming fragmented and has created a spiritual void in many of you. This emptiness triggers unrest and so upsets the status quo in order for a new era to emerge.

Strong feelings become contagious creating a collective wave of consciousness powerful enough to bring about change. The frequency of this wave of consciousness has the ability to drown out the present status quo if the majority of the masses affirm strongly the new ideology. Those who have lost belief in the present status quo will either submit to the new ideology that is being carried through on this wave of consciousness due to forced resonance (stronger vibration dominating a weaker one and influencing it to change its frequency) or they will rebel. In this case conflict will result until one force succumbs to the other. This is the energy pattern emerging in the Middle East.

There are other regions in the world where the collective consciousness of the masses has become far removed from their spiritual identity. This has caused an imbalance in the energies of those regions. You all need to work with your spiritual nature whilst reincarnated. If you do not it hinders your progress whilst here. Therefore if your material responsibilities, possessions and status are retarding your spiritual growth they will be stripped away. Economic recessions are an example of this process. As a consequence you may for the first time in your lives empathise with others who have always had less than yourselves. Other spiritual gifts that can be gained are, for example: humility, co-operation, compassion, adaptability in order to grow and an appreciation for the resources you do have. It is hoped you will learn never to place your faith in material things, as they are fleeting. Real security and happiness lies in working for the greater good of everyone. You cannot serve the self alone. Alternatively you may chose to become bitter, envious, angry and even hateful. However, these states of being need to be purged in the school of life.

Natural catastrophes are created by imbalances of energies. Having no material shackles in a national catastrophe enables the masses to focus on each other's survival and the safety of the shared environment. Working collectively together they bring about stability and security more quickly. Self-interests are diminished. This provides the opportunity for a nation to rebalance its material desires with its spiritual needs.

When a nation works together through a catastrophe self-interests are diminished. This unity of action and thought galvanises universal service for the greater good of all. It demotes the importance of material greed and unbalanced technological advancement. This accelerates opportunities to develop spiritual gifts which in turn aid its peoples' progress.

For the first time I was able to understand that natural unrest and material insecurities help us to reconnect with our spiritual priorities. We are able to align with our divine natures to bring about global changes that can impact the way we live our lives. This forces governments to make difficult decisions about how to bring about harmony, equality and balance. Such challenging global hardships have a spiritual correcting mechanism to bring about balance in ourselves.

Grace

I had been feeling sorry for myself last night before I slept. I had been invited out on a shopping trip the next day but had declined. My disposable income was virtually nothing. Every purchase had to be essential and accounted for. I would have liked to have bought myself a few summer tops or a summer dress. My wardrobe at the moment was very drab and I had resorted to mending clothes I once would have thrown out. My self-esteem was low as a result and I found myself crying and praying for my finances to improve, before I finally nodded off to sleep with sore eyes. Sunlight peeping through the gaps in my blinds woke me up. It was a new day and I was ashamed about being upset the night before. I was not starving; I had a roof over my head, a job, my health and people in my life who loved me. There were more important things in life than buying a few new clothes. I had been thoughtless and shallow.

Early afternoon arrived and I was enjoying a cup of tea having done some household chores earlier. There was a knock on the front door. It was Carmen who had invited me out on the shopping trip, the one I had declined. She had been de-cluttering her wardrobe the night before and had found four summer tops she had never worn. The tags were still attached. I tried them on and they all fitted. I was grateful and thanked her. Carmen then delved excitedly into her shopping bags showing me what she had bought. She had not tried on any of her purchases, so a mini fashion show proceeded. There was one item that did not fit her. It was a beautiful pink summer dress. I asked if I could try it on and she said yes. It fitted perfectly. Carmen then suggested I should keep the dress as an early Christmas present. I hugged her uncontrollably letting out a huge screech of joy. It did feel like Christmas had arrived early even though it was the middle of August! After she left I sat on my sofa smiling from ear to ear. If

I were a light bulb my luminosity would have lit up the entire city. I had to ask myself if this was a coincidence or had the universe deliberately given me what I had cried for the night before?

Having been brought up as a Christian I knew of the Book of Psalms. I had enjoyed reading it when I had attended church many years ago, as it read like poetry to me. I could hear in the recesses of my mind my mother singing the 23rd Psalm. "The Lord's my Shepherd I'll not want..." She had had a lovely voice. There was a claim that there was a Psalm for every human problem possible and that we could read it in our `hour of need` for support, guidance and answers. I would put it to the test. Whilst fumbling frantically through my dishevelled bookshelves for my Bible, the number 21 came into my mind. This is the Psalm I will read, I thought. I found my small burgundy childhood Bible. Flicking through its pages I came across little messages I had scribbled to Vicky my cousin when sermons had been putting us to sleep. I could picture us as two eightyear-olds popping sweets into our mouths when no one was looking. I was very fond of Vicky, my very softly spoken cousin. I hadn't seen her for years and thought how great it would be to reconnect with her again. Turning the pages to Psalm 21 I read apprehensively the first couple of lines.

"The king shall joy in thy strength, O Lord; and in thy salvation how greatly shall he rejoice! Thou hast given him his heart's desire, and hast not withholden the request of his lips. Selah."

It was a `jaw-dropping` revelation. Why had this request been answered? Yet my requests to win the lottery went unanswered?

My Divine Self

When you pour out your heart in sincerity to the universe your guardians listen attentively. They feel your woes and share your joys, every step of the way. Each challenging situation you find yourself in provides you with the opportunity to learn lessons. Once you learn to put your material desires into perspective and count your blessings in any challenging situation you develop grace. Grace creates an aura around you to attract mercy, favour, kindness and leniency in situations outside your control. This comes as a result of you expunging your shallow natures. The more grace you receive the more this is evidence of your progress whilst reincarnated here. Nothing is bestowed on you that would excuse you from lessons you need to learn in order to progress.

Being in a state of grace is like wearing a medal. It bestows on its owners privileges of all kinds of benevolence, which others might describe as luck. Nothing is coincidental in your life, everything is ordered and synchronised.

I understood that grace was a state you could arrive at whilst reincarnated once you tried to align with your spiritual priorities. This meant daily challenges and frustrations would be more easily worked through. You would acquire a better ability to readily anchor support and guidance from many sources in the universe. It could be likened to having a host of "fringe benefits" based upon right action and right thinking for the greater good of all.

Prayer and Patience

Ever since I had begun tapping into spiritual insights through my writing, I had made a conscious effort to start praying. I felt stronger and more capable than at any point in my life. I had been praying for strength and for new opportunities in my working life. However, nothing had materialised. I felt like a drone bee. Maintaining the hive of life had become repetitive. Nevertheless I was still grateful I had my health and the means to make a living.

I had begun doing visualisations to empower myself and to keep me focused. I had learned that my thoughts were powerful. I would visualise my hands being cupped together and full of mud. This would represent my cares and worries. I would then empty the contents of my hands into a giant pair of hands directly in front of me. These giant hands would then disappear. I would then look at my own hands that were now spotless. I had handed over my troubles and my cares to God, the Great Divine. When I did this normally I felt great, but today I was restless and annoyed with myself. My impatience was getting the better of me. I needed some inspiration.

My Divine Self

You are not in a position to know what your future holds. Accept that you are being guided and supported every step of the way on your path. Your prayers are heard and your disappointments and triumphs seen. When you pray sincerely it is like a deafening siren that goes out into the spheres. It is always listened to and acted upon for your highest good. You pray for the wrong things and they are not answered accordingly. This is when you lose faith in the goodness of the Great Divine. You need to know that in such instances your **progress is being safeguarded.**

All is well and time does not stand still. Things are moving in and out of your life constantly at a pace you can cope with. Your progress is dependent on the actions of others who have to cross your path for their own progress. Therefore the time and pace has to be right for all. Your destinies are influenced and intertwined with the actions of others. *Patience is what you need to learn.* By praying ceaselessly you will find the strength and the ability to persevere until new doors of opportunity open for you.

I had never really thought about others when I came to focus on my immediate needs and desires. I could understand now why it was important that I started seeing myself as connected to others. Being patient was also crucial. The drone bee did not live a repetitive life after all. He carried out his duties purposefully. He knew the role he played was significant to the survival of the bee colony and not just himself.

I would never have guessed that an insect would have something to teach me!

Prostitution

I had been invited to a school friend's 50th birthday party. Ruth looked great. The years had not ravished her looks or her figure. She wore a figure-hugging silver sequined dress and as I entered the hall she was dancing with her twenty-six-year-old daughter. They looked like sisters, not mother and daughter. I waved at them over the din of the chatter and music; she pointed that I get a drink and help myself to the buffet.

I headed towards the buffet and in so doing I was accosted by Mr and Mrs Rogers. "Hello Mr and Mrs Rogers, it's good to see you," I said, embracing them both. "How are you keeping, Martha?" asked Mrs Rogers. Mr Rogers then abruptly interrupted, "My God! You do resemble your mother." "I'm good!" I said. "Not married yet?" enquired Mrs Rogers. "No, I'm not married," I replied, feeling embarrassed and changing the subject as quickly as possible. "How is Annette? Is she here?" I enquired. Mr and Mrs Rogers' smiley faces glazed over with blank expressions. "Is something wrong? Is Annette all right?" I asked frantically. Mrs Rogers then grabbed my hand and they both led me to the table they were sitting at.

Mr Rogers sat with his left hand under his chin and shook his head from side to side not making any eye contact initially. "She moved to Chelsea in London and met this nightclub owner. He seemed quite pleasant when she brought him home to meet us last year. He was taking her out to posh places and buying her nice things. Then she changed. She stopped calling us everyday and would not visit us. We were both very concerned. So I decided to jump on a train and surprise her with a visit. When I got to her house and rang the bell the door was opened by a lady dressed in a flimsy night-dress. She smiled and pulled me through the door by my jacket lapel saying she was expecting me. I pushed her hands off from my jacket and asked her what the hell was going on. I caused such a fuss she called out for her boss. To my horror Annette came down the stairs followed by her boyfriend. I went ballistic. To cut a long story short they're running a brothel. We haven't spoken to her since."

I was shocked. Annette had been quite "straight-laced." She had been a Sunday school teacher in the local Baptist Church. Her parents were devoted Christians, her father being a deacon. Annette had brought shame on them in the local community. I would have thought that at a time like this they may have found some comfort and guidance from their religion. I was sure the Bible mentioned something about us not being able to notice a speck in our neighbour's eye if we had a beam in our own, or something like that. I was then called over by a school friend who was serving on the buffet to get something to eat. I made my excuses and left Mr and Mrs Rogers, telling them not to give up on Annette.

During the evening several others mentioned what Annette was now doing. It was quite a scandal. Some thought nothing was wrong with it, whilst some thought it was outrageous. I thought that Annette's choice had to be respected. This was the job she wanted to do. Was she wrong?

My Divine Self

A sexual relation is an exchange on many levels. At the most basic level your lustful and passionate natures are satisfied. At the worst extreme you dominate, subjugate and debase. On the other hand the act of consoling, supporting, cherishing and loving another through sex opens up a gateway to your beloved. In so doing an exchange of energy is ushered in by your feelings and this bestows an exhilarating deep healing through all your energy centres. It clears out any dross and leaves you invigorated and elated. A profound joy is experienced from connecting with another in this way, for you have been party to one another's healing. The exchange and the effect has been a sacred one, as it is when you procreate.

But sex is also is a vice for many who have not yet been able to access the spiritual experience because of their crude natures (spiritual backwardness). Prostitution acts as a conduit through which these basic needs can be processed. Those who service these basic needs are working through karmas whereby in past lives sexual depravity and immorality hindered their spiritual progress. It is hoped that wisdom will filter through to their consciousness to encourage their sexual natures to work in a more balanced and healing way in their present reincarnation. There are also `rescuers` who work in the sex industry. They are evolved individuals who are dedicated to helping prostitutes (and those who use their services) to change. In past lives they too had unbalanced sexual tendencies but overcame them.

As a consequence of many of you being spiritually backward with crude natures, prostitution will continue to exist. It will also attract other vices. However, all hope is not lost as mankind constantly progresses.

I had to admit sex had always been better with partners I genuinely felt love for. Other exchanges left me feeling dirty, exhausted, feeling rotten or even violated. As I had got older my sexual exchanges only took place with a partner I had love for. One-night-stands were not for me now.

Was it possible that Annette was one of these rescuers? However, as a society we needed to put more support in place to protect and help sex workers.

The One

I opened the front door. It was Ben. I looked into his hazel-green eyes as he threw his arms around me and planted a big wet kiss on my mouth. We embraced for a few seconds and then our lips parted. GOD! How I loved him. When he held me I felt safe and loved. He was 6ft and 3" tall and he was my `rock`. He was bright, witty, funny, passionate, caring, kind, respectful and genuine. I loved the bones of this man. He was not the type of guy I would have normally gone for. He was fair and normally I liked my men to be dark. Also he was like a big teddy bear. In the past I had gone for the lean and athletic type. Ben was Gemini, an air sign, and I was keen on fire signs. For once I was glad a train had been delayed, as we had met on a train platform as a result. There were more things to like about him than there were to dislike. Luckily he thought the same about me. We were like a hand in a glove. We fitted each other perfectly.

Ben had come over to have tea with me and was mindful of the time. He had a report to check before he went to bed that night for a business meeting the next day. It was 10. 00 pm and looking at his watch he said he had to go. We parted the same way we had greeted that evening with a hug and a kiss. As I closed the door behind Ben I could say the man of my dreams had been packaged as him. He had been worth the thirty-nine year wait. Good things did come to those who wait.

The Formula

As I entered the car park I was careful to make sure I parked in my designated space. I had heard they were quite strict about that here. I wanted to make a good impression on my first day in my new job. I was very excited. I was to be in charge of a team of six in the payroll department for the local council. It was just the right challenge I needed. My team introduced themselves to me and they all seemed nice and professional.

When I arrived home that evening I was very contented. My life was running very smoothly. Upon sitting down on my sofa I realised I was sitting on something hard. I stood up pulling my pad from beneath me. My first instinct was to throw it on my side table and reach for the remote control for the tv. I hadn't written in my notepad for months but I found myself holding it carefully. Pages were falling out of it, it was torn and tatty yet the formula for alchemy was to be found on its pages. My body, mind and spirit had been transformed by its contents. Strangely enough, the pad now resembled how I once felt. I became emotional. This pad was making me cry! But they were tears of heartfelt gratitude. I found myself opening it up and writing the following:

- You are responsible for your own actions, progress and state of wellbeing.

- Be kind and respectful to yourself, others and all living things.

- You must believe to receive and that means always have hope and faith.

- Everyone is your teacher and the best lessons are the hardest as they provide the greatest gifts.

- Be positive and work with what you have.

- Sometimes going with the flow is the best thing to do when opportunities don't present themselves. It is hard work swimming against the flow of a current but patience is always rewarded.

- Don't live selfishly but purposefully as what you do affects everyone else.

- Be gracious in whatever situation you find yourself in. Do not let anyone "rattle you." Things are in a state of constant progress.

- We truly reap what we sow.

- Material possessions and status don't "make us," but signal that we have a greater responsibility towards others.

- Don't be afraid to have conversations with yourself or to pray to a deity you believe in. Spirit is always listening in. Give thanks and ask for the support you need.

- Loving yourself is not enough; it needs to be shared. More importantly we are Divine Beings loved beyond human capacity. We are not marooned here without a support network.

This is what I had learned. It had given rise to an empowered and more fulfilled Martha Thompson than at any other point in my life. I then heard the following:

My Divine Self

Your life here is a school of progress and it is up to you to attend and pass your lessons. Upon doing so you graduate and ascend the hierarchy of progress. Your studies cannot be rushed and so all of you reincarnate many times over. Other planes of progress exist for you to aspire to. So it is important that you learn to work with your divine natures no matter what school of progress you attend. The more you pass in your studies the easier it is for you to assimilate greater truths of the universe, and your lives become more fulfilling. Nothing can stop you from progressing but yourself. The universe is bountiful and wishes to furnish you with all that you need for your highest good; you only need to believe to receive the guidance and support for them to materialise in your lives.

We all co-exist in a universal web and the action of one reverberates throughout the universe. Therefore it is important that your actions are honourable as the repercussions are felt by all. You are made up of the essence of the Great Divine and are divine beings so let nothing thwart you as you are capable of much and lack nothing.

(My name is Ellis. I am one of your guides. A spiritual teacher who will give you counsel if you will listen.)

That voice I had heard that had told me to "get a grip" had been Ellis. If he had revealed himself to me earlier I would have freaked out. I would have blocked out what I was writing. He had encouraged me to acknowledge my divine self and see my life from a spiritual perspective. Ellis had empowered me and enabled me to access spiritual truths I had lost in my physical reality. I was now also able to listen to him and I could avoid the quicksand effect.

Like a phoenix rising from the ashes of my former self I could fly higher and further than I could ever have imagined. Life would never wear me down again.

P. S. I forgot to tell you that your own insights will also surface and you will see life's challenges as gifts.

Wishing you peace in your heart and mind.

Martha x

BOOKS

O is a symbol of the world, of oneness and unity. In different cultures it also means the "eye," symbolizing knowledge and insight. We aim to publish books that are accessible, constructive and that challenge accepted opinion, both that of academia and the "moral majority."

Our books are available in all good English language bookstores worldwide. If you don't see the book on the shelves ask the bookstore to order it for you, quoting the ISBN number and title. Alternatively you can order online (all major online retail sites carry our titles) or contact the distributor in the relevant country, listed on the copyright page.

See our website **www.o-books.net** for a full list of over 500 titles, growing by 100 a year.

And tune in to myspiritradio.com for our book review radio show, hosted by June-Elleni Laine, where you can listen to the authors discussing their books.

mySpiritRadio